THE FASTENER EMPIRE

How the Smallest Part
Decides the Biggest Win

THE FASTENER EMPIRE

How the Smallest Part
Decides the Biggest Win

DHRUV KHANDELWAL

Worldwide Published by
Pendown Press

PENDOWN PRESS LLP

An ISO 9001 & ISO 14001 Certified Co.,

Regd. Office: 3767A, Kanhaiya Nagar,

Tri Nagar, Delhi-110035

Ph.: 8130886000, 9650072927

E-mail: info@pendownpress.com

Branch Office: 1A/2A, 20, Hari Sadan, Ansari Road,

Daryaganj, New Delhi-110002

Ph.: 011-45794768

Website: PendownPress.com

Edition: 2025

Price: ₹ 499

ISBN: 978-93-6338-610-5

Layout and Cover Designed by Pendown Graphics Team

Printed and Bound in India by Thomson Press India Ltd.

Contents

Chapter 1

Setting Context The How & Why of This Book

In the world of machines, every component has a role—but not every role is given its due respect.

Fasteners— those seemingly insignificant, screws, nuts, bolts and washers—are often overshadowed by the grander, more glamorous elements of mechanical design.

They're small, cheap, and almost invisible in the final product. But their importance? That's where most manufacturers go wrong, their impact is immense and critical.

Behind every functioning piece of machinery is a promise of peak and premium performance that can only come true if held together by the right fasteners that connect, secure, and stabilize.

Yet, these unsung heroes are frequently treated as an afterthought. Too often, we choose fasteners based on cost or availability, not realizing that the wrong choice, even by a small margin, can lead to vibration issues, structural fatigue, leaks, breakdowns, or worse. These consequences don't always appear immediately, but when they do, they can be costly, dangerous, and sometimes catastrophic, resulting in shutdowns and major loss of productivity and, hence, profit.

This book is a wake-up call.

It doesn't just explain what fasteners are or how they work—it shows why they matter.

Whether you're a designer, an engineer, a maintenance technician, or a decision-maker, you'll come to understand that using the right fastener isn't just a technical detail; it's a critical decision that can make or break a machine, a project, or even a business.

This book is a culmination of my experiences and learnings in the fasteners industry, written with a singular goal: to help OEMs and manufacturers make better, more informed decisions. Fasteners are often overlooked, yet they are mission-critical components that directly influence manufacturing efficiency, product quality, and operational costs.

Beyond identifying the challenges associated with fasteners, this book provides actionable solutions. It delves into the hidden impact of fasteners on your operations and offers guidance on optimizing their use for maximum efficiency, reliability, and cost-effectiveness. Whether it's improving fastener selection, ensuring supply chain stability, or preventing production failures, the insights in this book are designed to help you avoid costly mistakes.

You'll discover how the right choices can improve reliability, safety, and longevity, and how poor decisions, though they might seem minor at first, can lead to massive losses. With practical insights, real-world examples, and clear explanations, this book sheds light on the true value of fasteners and empowers you to make smarter, more informed choices.

Because when it comes to engineering, it's not just about what holds the spotlight—it's about what holds everything together and tight!

If this book can help even one manufacturer streamline their operations or avoid a production failure, it will have fulfilled its purpose.

Chapter 2

Who Am I & How Am I So Confident of This?

I am a fourth-generation entrepreneur in the fasteners industry, with three generations of my family still actively contributing to this field. For me, fasteners are not just a business—they are a legacy and a passion that runs in my blood. My family's journey in this industry spans over a century, with roots that trace back to the time before India gained independence.

My father, Mr. Mukesh Khandelwal, ventured into manufacturing the same year I was born. During my early years, I was raised in our factory, which also doubled as our residence. It was where I took my first steps, surrounded by the rhythmic hum of machines and the sight of fasteners being meticulously crafted. Growing up surrounded by machines and fasteners, I developed a deep fascination for them. This passion inspired me to pursue mechanical engineering—the science behind fasteners. While I have spent the last ten years working full-time in this industry, it feels as though I have been a part of it since birth.

It was my father who taught me that fasteners are more than just tiny components—they are the backbone of operations, holding together the innovations of entire industries. He was not just a manufacturer; he was a visionary and a natural marketeer. I was always in awe of how he could walk into a room and instantly build trust with customers. He never sold products—he built relationships.

His favorite saying, one I've carried with me throughout my journey, was:

"A small component can make a big difference."

This simple yet profound line encapsulates the essence of the fasteners industry and serves as the guiding principle for this book.

For decades, my father poured his heart into building Empire Fasteners into a trusted name for OEMs across India. From naming the brand to marketing it tirelessly across the country, he was relentless in his pursuit of excellence. His dedication is the foundation on which I've built my career and my new chapter with our company, **Raj Industries**, and brand GYPDRIVE®.

For many years, I worked in my family's business, Empire Fasteners, catering to India's top OEMs. However, in an unexpected twist of fate, a year ago, my life took a sudden turn. After a family division, I had to start over from scratch in the same field but in an entirely different territory.

The split meant I lost everything—

- The Brand Name
- The Customers
- The Team I had built
- Even the Comfort of Familiar Surroundings.

I left my home and moved to a city where I had never worked before, among people who didn't know me, and I began building a new identity.

I believed that a decade of experience in the industry would help me quickly rebuild, but the reality was far more challenging. It was an uphill battle to run a new factory, Raj Industries and a new brand, GYPDRIVE®, gain customers, and establish myself again.

There were days when the struggle felt insurmountable, and I questioned whether I should continue at all. **The only thing that kept me going was the unshakable support of my father. He stood by me through every setback, encouraging me to persevere. Today, Raj Industries is named after my grandfather, Mr. Raj Nath Gupta—the man whose vision and hard work laid the foundation for our family's journey in this industry. His name represents integrity, precision, and a commitment to excellence. My mission with Raj Industries is not just to carry forward their legacy but to expand it**

I am deeply grateful to my mother, Ratna Khandelwal, and my wife, Kanika Khandelwal, for always supporting and motivating me. Their belief in me has been my greatest strength and a constant source of encouragement during challenging times.

However, as the wise say, and I experienced firsthand, every disaster is a blessing in disguise.

During this journey, I took the opportunity to focus on skills I hadn't been able to prioritize earlier.

I met new people, expanded my knowledge of different products, and gained fresh perspectives. One conversation, in particular, left a profound impact on me.

I had the privilege of meeting a scientist who had been part of India's historic lunar exploration project— The Chandrayaan-3 mission.

As we spoke, I was astonished to learn that despite India's advancements in technology, the mission still relied on imported

fasteners. Even after decades of progress, we had not localized this crucial component.

That moment opened my eyes.

I realized how far we still had to go to achieve true self-reliance in manufacturing.

It became clear to me that our mission must be bigger than just serving India; we must aim to compete with the world's leading economies. We must make in India, for India, and for the world. I had the privilege of contributing to this vision as a member of the BIS standard drafting committee, where I worked to refine India's national standards to align with global requirements. This opportunity was both an honor and a responsibility, as it allowed me to actively shape the future of the industry.

In line with this commitment, **Raj Industries achieved a significant milestone by being awarded India's first-ever BIS license for drywall screws.** This accomplishment is not just a testament to our dedication but also a step towards positioning India as a global leader in fastener manufacturing.

This realization became my mission: to bring fastener manufacturing in India to global standards. My goal is to make every fastener available locally, eliminating dependency on imports.

This book is an extension of that mission.

I can't personally reach every manufacturer and OEM, but through this book, I am sharing the knowledge and insights I have gained over the years.

While working on my book, I was blessed with a baby boy, Rudra Raj Khandelwal. His name is a tribute to my grandfather, and though he is only a few weeks old, he inspires me to work harder every day. He reminds me of the legacy I carry and the future I am building for him and the generations to come.

This journey has not been easy, but it has been deeply fulfilling. With the unwavering support of my family and the lessons I've learned from my struggles, I am more determined than ever to make a difference in this industry.

For me, this is not just about fasteners—it's about contributing to India's self-reliance and global leadership.

It is heartening to see that my mission is in full swing when clients have things like this to say. It makes me work with double energy.

From Mere Preferred Vendor to Trusted Advisor

Dhruv Khandelwal is a visionary in the fasteners industry, blending his technical expertise with an unwavering commitment to quality and innovation. His ability to understand our unique needs and deliver customized solutions has significantly improved our operations. More than a supplier, he is a trusted advisor who prioritizes long-term partnerships. His passion for his craft is inspiring, and his work consistently exceeds expectations.

Chapter 3

Inside the Screw: The Science OEMs Should Know

To be good at anything, you must have thorough knowledge of that domain/industry. So, of course, mastery over fasteners means first understanding the types of fasteners, their uses, and the materials they are made of.

Over the past ten years, I've worked with various types of fasteners, each serving specific purposes across industries. While the market offers an extensive range of options, this section highlights the commonly used fasteners, categorized for ease of understanding.

A. Different Types of Heads

1. Truss Head

- **Description:** The truss head is a low-profile, dome-shaped head with a wide surface area.
- **Purpose:** Primarily used to prevent material deformation while fastening thin materials.
- **Applications:** Ideal for securing sheet metal, electrical panels, or lightweight assemblies.
- **Advantages:** The broad surface area helps distribute the load evenly, preventing the material from tearing.

2. **Binding Head**

- **Description:** This head features a flat top with a thicker base under the screw's head.
- **Purpose:** Secures soft or fragile materials without causing damage.
- **Applications:** Frequently used in binding documents, electrical wiring, or plastic assemblies.
- **Advantages:** Its design prevents overtightening and protects delicate materials.

3. **Pan Head**

- **Description:** A rounded top with a flat underside that sits above the material's surface.
- **Purpose:** Provides a robust and aesthetically appealing fastener for a range of applications.
- **Applications:** Common in woodworking, furniture, and light-duty metal assemblies.
- **Advantages:** Ensures excellent tool engagement and a smooth, polished finish.

4. **Countersunk (FLAT) Head**

- **Description:** Conical head designed to sit flush or below the material's surface.
- **Purpose:** Eliminates protrusions for a smooth, finished look and reduces drag in applications like aerospace or automotive.
- **Applications:** Common in flat panel assemblies, furniture, and situations requiring concealed fasteners.
- **Advantages:** The countersunk profile minimizes the risk of snagging or interference.

6. **Brazier Head**
   - **Description:** A large domed top with a slightly flattened profile.
   - **Purpose:** Provides a large bearing surface to spread the load over a wider area.
   - **Applications:** Used in aircraft assembly, high-tension structures, and automotive body panels.
   - **Advantages:** Excellent strength and resistance to pull-through in lightweight materials.
7. **Cheese Head**
   - **Description:** A cylindrical head with straight sides and a flat seating surface.
   - **Purpose:** Allows for deep screwdriver engagement for high-torque applications.
   - **Applications:** Found in electrical and mechanical applications requiring precision.
   - **Advantages:** Provides excellent torque transmission and easy alignment during installation.
8. **Hexagon Washer Head**
   - **Description:** Combines a hexagonal head with an integrated washer base.
   - **Purpose:** Distributes the load evenly and resists loosening under vibration.
   - **Applications:** Widely used in automotive and industrial applications.
   - **Advantages:** Eliminates the need for separate washers, reducing assembly time.

9. **Oval Head**

- **Description:** A hybrid between a countersunk and a round head with a slightly domed top.
- **Purpose:** Offers a decorative finish while maintaining a low-profile design.
- **Applications:** Decorative furniture, light fixtures, and precision woodworking.
- **Advantages:** Combines functionality and aesthetics for exposed surfaces.

10. **Round Head**

- **Description:** Fully domed head with no flat underside.
- **Purpose:** Provides a smooth finish and low-profile fastening.
- **Applications:** Used in furniture, household appliances, and light-duty assemblies.
- **Advantages:** Protects against tampering and provides a visually appealing look.

11. **Button Head (Socket/Allen)**

- **Description:** Low-profile cylindrical head with a rounded top.
- **Purpose:** Ideal for compact applications requiring high torque.
- **Applications:** Robotics, machinery, and industrial equipment.
- **Advantages:** The Allen drive reduces tool slippage and ensures a clean, professional finish.

12. **Pan Framing Head**

- **Description:** Wide, flat head with a slight dome for framing applications.

- **Purpose:** Provides excellent holding power in construction.
- **Applications:** Used in structural assemblies and metal-to-wood connections.
- **Advantages:** The flat underside ensures maximum material contact.

13. **Hexagon Head**
    - **Description:** Standard six-sided head.
    - **Purpose:** Allows for high torque and secure fastening.
    - **Applications:** Universal applications in automotive, construction, and heavy machinery.
    - **Advantages:** Can be tightened with a wrench or socket for added convenience.

B. Different Types of Screw Drivers

1. **Philips**
    - **Description:** A cross-shaped recess in the screw head.
    - **Purpose:** Provides better torque control and reduces slippage.
    - **Applications:** Widely used in electronics, automotive, and construction.
    - **Advantages:** Self-centering design minimizes cam-out (slipping).
2. **Six Lobe**
    - **Description:** Star-shaped drive designed for high torque applications.
    - **Purpose:** Prevents stripping and provides maximum torque transfer.
    - **Applications:** Automotive, aerospace, and precision equipment.

- **Advantages:** High durability and resistance to wear.

3. **Slotted**

  - **Description:** A simple, straight-line recess in the screw head.
  - **Purpose:** Easy to use with basic tools.
  - **Applications:** Traditional woodworking and household applications.
  - **Advantages:** Readily available and cost-effective.

4. **Philips Slotted**

  - **Description:** Combination of Philips and slotted drives.
  - **Purpose:** Offers versatility for multiple tool types.
  - **Applications:** Electrical fixtures and consumer goods.
  - **Advantages:** Reduces the need for specialized tools.

5. **Y Type**

  - **Description:** A three-pronged drive system.
  - **Purpose:** Provides secure engagement and reduces stripping.
  - **Applications:** Used in electronics like video game consoles and laptops.
  - **Advantages:** Increased resistance to tampering.

6. **Tri-Wing**

  - **Description:** A three-winged shape, often used in tamper-proof screws.
  - **Purpose:** Prevents unauthorized removal.
  - **Applications:** Aerospace and consumer electronics.
  - **Advantages:** Secure and specialized.

7. **Pozi-Driv**
    - **Description:** An enhanced Philips design with additional grip features.
    - **Purpose:** Provides extra torque without cam-out.
    - **Applications:** Electrical systems and heavy-duty construction.
    - **Advantages:** Ideal for high-torque applications.
8. **Hexagon Socket (Allen)**
    - **Description:** Hexagonal recess in the screw head.
    - **Purpose:** Allows high torque application without damaging the drive.
    - **Applications:** Bicycles, furniture, and machinery.
    - **Advantages:** Compact design for tight spaces.
9. **Triangle**
    - **Description:** Triangular-shaped recess for tamper-proof screws.
    - **Purpose:** Offers high security and prevents unauthorized removal.
    - **Applications:** Childproof toys and industrial equipment.
    - **Advantages:** Requires a specialized tool for operation.
10. **Square**
    - **Description:** Square-shaped drive recess.
    - **Purpose:** Provides better torque control and reduces slipping.
    - **Applications:** Construction and woodworking.
    - **Advantages:** Highly durable and user-friendly.
11. **Slot Indented**
    - **Description:** A slotted drive with slight recessing.

- **Purpose:** Increases surface grip for improved torque.
- **Applications:** Specialty hardware and automotive.
- **Advantages:** Reduces wear during repeated use.

12. Spline

- **Description:** Star-like design with multiple teeth.
- **Purpose:** Distributes torque evenly across multiple points.
- **Applications:** Aerospace and precision machinery.
- **Advantages:** Prevents deformation under stress.

13. 5 Point/8 Point

- **Description:** Unique designs with five or eight contact points.
- **Purpose:** Tamper-proof designs for high-security applications.
- **Applications:** Defense and sensitive equipment.
- **Advantages:** Enhances security and prevents tampering.

14. H Type

- **Description:** High-strength recess for industrial screws.
- **Purpose:** Ensures high torque transfer without slippage.
- **Applications:** Heavy machinery and industrial tools.
- **Advantages:** Ideal for high-load applications.

15. Philips Slot Indented

- **Description:** A hybrid design combining Philips with a recessed slot.
- **Purpose:** Provides versatile torque application and ease of use.
- **Applications:** Electrical, construction, and automotive industries.
- **Advantages:** Reduces wear and enhances longevity.

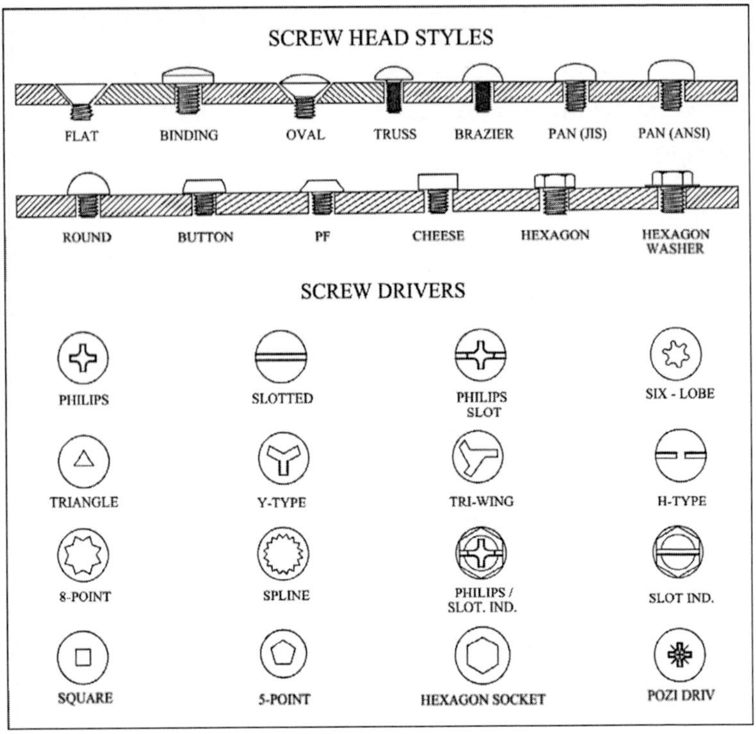

C. Different Types of Threads

1. AB Type Thread

- **Description:** A thread design combining the sharp, pointed end of Type A with the finer threading of Type B.
- **Purpose:** Offers superior starting power in hard or thin materials and strong thread engagement.
- **Applications:** Used in sheet metal, plastics, and light metal assemblies.
- **Advantages:** Balances ease of use with durability, suitable for various substrates.

2. **A Type Thread**
   - **Description:** Coarse-threaded design with a sharp point.
   - **Purpose:** Penetrates softer materials like wood, thin plastics, or low-density metals.
   - **Applications:** Commonly used in woodworking and light-duty applications.
   - **Advantages:** Quick installation with minimal resistance.
3. **B Type Thread**
   - **Description:** Coarse threaded design without a sharp point.
   - **Purpose:** Designed for pre-tapped holes in hard materials like metal.
   - **Applications:** For light and heavy sheet metal non-ferrous castings, plastics, impregnated plywoods, asbestos combinations, and other materials.
   - **Advantages:** Larger root diameter with finer thread pitch.
4. **F Type Thread**
   - **Description:** A thread cutting screw with machine screw thread with blunt tapered point, have multi-cutting edges and chip cavities.
   - **Purpose:** Ideal for heavy-duty fastening.
   - **Applications:** Automotive, heavy machinery, and industrial use.
   - **Advantages:** High strength and stability under load.
5. **BT Type Thread**
   - **Description:** A thread cutting screw with B type thread.
   - **Purpose:** Used for fast assembly in materials requiring less thread engagement.

- **Applications:** For plastics and other soft materials with large chip-clearing and cutting edges.
- **Advantages:** Provides quick fastening with minimal material displacement.

6. **U Type Thread**
    - **Description:** A unique thread pattern designed for specific applications.
    - **Purpose:** Enhances holding strength in specialized materials.
    - **Applications:** Often seen in HVAC and plumbing applications.
    - **Advantages:** Customized for niche industry requirements.
7. **Machine Screws (mm/BSF/BSW/UNC/UNF)**
    - **Description:** Precision threads available in metric (mm) and imperial standards (BSF, BSW, UNC, UNF).
    - **Purpose:** Secure components in machinery and electronics with high precision.
    - **Applications:** Found in automotive, aerospace, and consumer electronics.
    - **Advantages:** Wide availability of sizes for tailored fits.
8. **Wood Screws**
    - **Description:** Coarse-threaded screws designed for wood.
    - **Purpose:** Provides a strong grip on wood without splitting it.
    - **Applications:** Furniture assembly, carpentry, and woodworking.
    - **Advantages:** Easy to drive and resistant to loosening over time.

9. **Chipboard Screws**
    - **Description:** Thin, sharp threads for engineered wood products.
    - **Purpose:** Designed for particleboard, MDF, and chipboard.
    - **Applications:** Modular furniture and cabinetry.
    - **Advantages:** Prevents splitting and provides superior holding power.

10. **Drywall Screws**
    - **Description:** Screws with deep threads designed for drywall.
    - **Purpose:** Secure drywall to wooden or metal studs.
    - **Applications:** Construction and renovation projects.
    - **Advantages:** Easy to drive with minimal damage to drywall.

11. **Self-Drilling Screws**
    - **Description:** Screws with a drill bit-like tip.
    - **Purpose:** Eliminates the need for pre-drilling in metal or wood.
    - **Applications:** HVAC, roofing, and industrial construction.
    - **Advantages:** Saves time and ensures precise drilling.

13. **PT Thread**
    - **Description:** Threads designed for plastic applications.
    - **Purpose:** Creates a secure fastening in plastics without cracking.
    - **Applications:** Consumer electronics and appliances.
    - **Advantages:** Ensures high resistance to loosening in plastics.

14. CA Thread

- **Description:** Thread forming screws with coarse or fine pitch machine screws threads.
- **Purpose:** Designed for high-retention fastening.
- **Applications:** Aerospace and high-performance engineering.
- **Advantages:** Useful where holes between two adjoining pieces of sheet metal may be somewhat misaligned.

14. Triangular Threads

- **Description: Tri-lobular screws**.
- **Purpose:** Eliminates tapping of unthreaded holes.
- **Applications:** Automotive, Electronics, Appliances, etc
- **Advantages:** Does not produce chips in an untapped hole and drives less torque.

SCREW THREAD STYLES

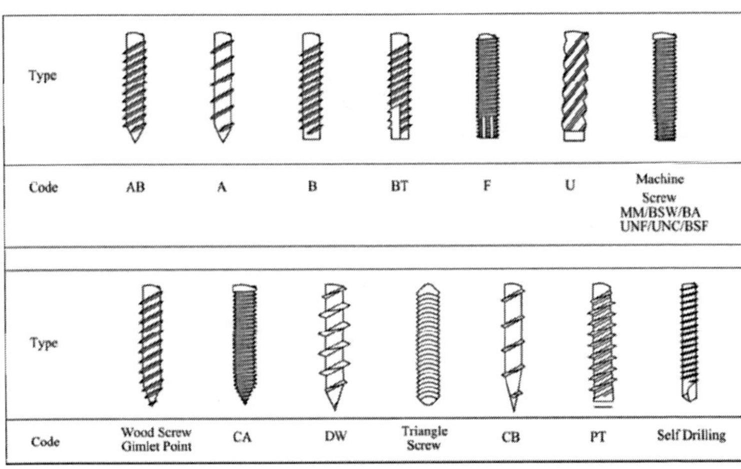

D. Different Types of Coatings

1. **Zinc Trivalent Plating (White, Yellow, Black)**
    - **Purpose:** Corrosion resistance for mild to moderate environments.
    - **Applications:** Automotive, furniture, and electronics.
    - **Advantages:** Environmentally friendly, available in various finishes.
2. **Zinc Iron Plating**
    - **Purpose:** Offers enhanced corrosion resistance with added strength.
    - **Applications:** Automotive and heavy machinery.
    - **Advantages:** Combines durability with long-term protection.
3. **Zinc Nickel Plating**
    - **Purpose:** Superior corrosion resistance in extreme conditions.
    - **Applications:** Marine, automotive, and aerospace industries.
    - **Advantages:** High durability in saline environments.
4. **Zinc Aluminium Flake Coating**
    - **Purpose:** High-performance coating for extreme corrosion resistance.
    - **Applications:** Bridges, wind turbines, automobiles, and outdoor structures.
    - **Advantages:** Long-lasting and eco-friendly.

5. **Nickel Plating**
    - **Purpose:** Adds wear resistance and aesthetic appeal.
    - **Applications:** Consumer goods and decorative hardware.
    - **Advantages:** Combines function with aesthetics.
6. **Tin Plating**
    - **Purpose:** Enhances solderability and corrosion resistance.
    - **Applications:** Electrical connectors and circuit boards.
    - **Advantages:** Easy to apply and cost-effective.
7. **Brass Plating**
    - **Purpose:** Adds a decorative finish and moderate corrosion resistance.
    - **Applications:** Furniture hardware and ornamental fasteners.
    - **Advantages:** Combines strength with a classic look.
8. **Electropolishing Stainless Steel**
    - **Purpose:** Removes surface imperfections and enhances corrosion resistance.
    - **Applications:** Medical, food-grade, and marine industries.
    - **Advantages:** Creates a smooth, shiny surface.
9. **Hot Dip Galvanizing**
    - **Purpose:** Provides a thick, durable zinc coating for outdoor protection.
    - **Applications:** Construction and agricultural equipment.
    - **Advantages:** Long-lasting and cost-efficient for large-scale use.
10. **Phosphating**
    - **Purpose:** Prepares metal surfaces for painting or coating.

- **Applications:** Automotive, construction, and industrial equipment.
- **Advantages:** Improves adhesion and corrosion resistance.

11. **Powder Coating**

- **Purpose:** Durable, weather-resistant finish available in various colors.
- **Applications:** Outdoor furniture, appliances, and vehicles.
- **Advantages:** Eco-friendly and visually appealing.

12. **PTFE (Teflon/Xylan)**

- **Purpose:** Reduces friction and adds non-stick properties.
- **Applications:** Aerospace, automotive, and food-grade equipment.
- **Advantages:** High resistance to chemicals and wear.

E. Raw Materials Used in Fasteners

The choice of raw material for a fastener is crucial as it directly impacts its strength, corrosion resistance, and suitability for specific applications. Below is a detailed overview of common materials used in fastener manufacturing:

1. **Carbon Steel**

- **Grades:** Low, medium, and high carbon steel.
- **Characteristics:**
  - Low cost and high availability.
  - Moderate strength and ductility.
- **Applications:** General-purpose fasteners, including screws, bolts, and nuts for construction and machinery.

- **Advantages:**
  - Easily machined and heat-treated.
  - Versatile for various coatings to improve performance.

2. **Stainless Steel**
   - **Grades:** 304, 316, 410, etc.
   - **Characteristics:**
     - High corrosion resistance, especially in marine or chemical environments.
     - Non-magnetic (in some grades).
   - **Applications:**
     - Food processing, medical devices, and marine equipment.
   - **Advantages:**
     - Durable and long-lasting.
     - Aesthetic appeal with a shiny finish.

3. **Alloy Steel**
   - **Characteristics:**
     - Enhanced strength and hardness due to added alloys (chromium, molybdenum, etc.).
     - Superior wear resistance.
   - **Applications:**
     - Heavy-duty applications, such as automotive and industrial machinery.
   - **Advantages:**
     - Can withstand high stress and load.
     - Heat-treatable for improved mechanical properties.

4. **Brass**
   - **Characteristics:**
     - High corrosion resistance and good conductivity.
     - Soft and malleable, ideal for decorative applications.
   - **Applications:** Plumbing, electrical components, and decorative fasteners.
   - **Advantages:**
     - Aesthetic finish.
     - Resistant to tarnishing.
5. **Aluminum**
   - **Characteristics:**
     - Lightweight and corrosion-resistant.
     - Low tensile strength compared to steel.
   - **Applications:** Aerospace, electronics, and lightweight structures.
   - **Advantages:**
     - Excellent for weight-sensitive applications.
     - Non-magnetic and recyclable.
6. **Titanium**
   - **Characteristics:**
     - High strength-to-weight ratio.
     - Exceptional corrosion resistance, even in extreme environments.
   - **Applications:** Aerospace, medical implants, and high-performance vehicles.
   - **Advantages:**
     - Biocompatible and non-toxic.
     - Resistant to high temperatures.

7. **Copper**
   - **Characteristics:**
     - Excellent thermal and electrical conductivity.
     - Natural corrosion resistance.
   - **Applications:** Electrical components, roofing fasteners, and plumbing.
   - **Advantages:**
     - Long lifespan and high ductility.
8. **Nylon and Plastics**
   - **Characteristics:**
     - Lightweight and corrosion-free.
     - Non-conductive and chemically resistant.
   - **Applications:** Electronics, toys, and light-duty fixtures.
   - **Advantages:**
     - Flexible and cost-effective.
     - Reduces wear on mating surfaces.

F. Adhesives and Locking Mechanisms

Adhesives and locking mechanisms ensure the reliability and integrity of fastened joints, particularly in high-vibration or critical applications.

Thread Lockers

- **Description:** Anaerobic adhesives that secure threaded fasteners by curing in the absence of air.

- **Grades:**
  - **Low Strength:** For easy disassembly (e.g., electronic assemblies).
  - **Medium Strength:** For applications requiring moderate torque (e.g., home appliances).
  - **High Strength:** For permanent fastening (e.g., heavy machinery).
- **Applications:** Prevents loosening due to vibrations in automotive, aerospace, and machinery.
- **Advantages:**
  - Prevents leaks and corrosion.
  - Easy to apply and provides uniform clamping force.

Chapter 4

Choosing The Right Raw Material

Now that the previous chapter has provided thorough information on the types of the most commonly used fasteners, their raw materials, coatings, and locking mechanisms, etc. Now, the next step is to understand how to choose the raw material best suited to your requirements, as the foundation of performance lies in the material.

The raw material of a fastener isn't just a technical detail, it's the backbone of its performance. Choosing the right material can mean the difference between lasting strength and premature failure, between safety and risk, between profit and loss.

Every application places unique demands on a fastener, be it load-bearing capacity, exposure to harsh environments, aesthetic appeal, or the need for lightweight construction. A one-size-fits-all approach simply doesn't work.

This breaks down how different raw materials behave under various conditions and why selecting the right one is not just smart engineering, but essential for long-term reliability, efficiency, and safety. Whether you're working on industrial machines or delicate electronics, understanding your material choices is the first step toward building with confidence.

A. Strength and Load Requirements

➢ **High Loads or Heavy-Duty Applications:**

- Use **high-carbon steel** or **alloy steel** for their superior strength and durability.
- Common in automotive, construction, and industrial machinery.

➢ **Medium Loads:**

- Use **medium-carbon steel** or **stainless steel** for moderate strength and resistance to wear.
- Ideal for general machinery and household appliances.

➢ **Light Loads:**

- Use **aluminum**, **brass**, or **nylon** for lightweight and non-critical applications.
- Best for electronics and decorative purposes.

B. Environmental Factors

➢ **Corrosive Environments (e.g., marine or chemical exposure):**

- Use **stainless steel (316 grade)** for its exceptional corrosion resistance.
- **Titanium** is suitable for extreme corrosion resistance, especially in seawater.
- **Zinc-plated steel** provides a cost-effective option for moderate corrosion resistance.

➢ **High Temperatures:**

- Use **titanium** or **heat-treated alloy steel**.
- Suitable for aerospace and exhaust systems.

- **Non-Corrosive Indoor Environments:**
    - Use **low-carbon steel** for its cost-effectiveness.
    - Common in furniture and light-duty fixtures.

C. Aesthetic Requirements

- For visible fasteners in decorative applications, use:
    - **Brass** or **stainless steel** for a polished finish.
    - **Nickel-plated** or **powder-coated steel** for customizable aesthetics.

D. Weight Sensitivity

- Use **aluminum** or **nylon** for applications where weight reduction is crucial, such as aerospace, electronics, or lightweight structures.

Chapter 5

International Standards for Fasteners

In the world of fasteners, precision is everything, and that precision begins with standards.

Adhering to internationally recognized fastener standards is not just about ticking boxes or meeting regulations. It's about ensuring that every bolt, screw, or nut performs exactly as expected, every single time.

Compliance guarantees consistency in material quality, thread accuracy, coating thickness, and mechanical performance. It minimizes the risk of failure, enhances durability under stress, and ensures seamless integration across global supply chains.

Whether you're manufacturing heavy machinery, assembling vehicles, or constructing buildings, working with standardized fasteners means building with confidence, safety, and reliability at the core.

The global fastener industry relies on a range of international standards to ensure consistency, quality, and compatibility across different regions and industries. These standards define the specifications for materials, dimensions, threads, coatings, and performance requirements of fasteners.

Shared below is a table summarizing the major international standards used in various countries:

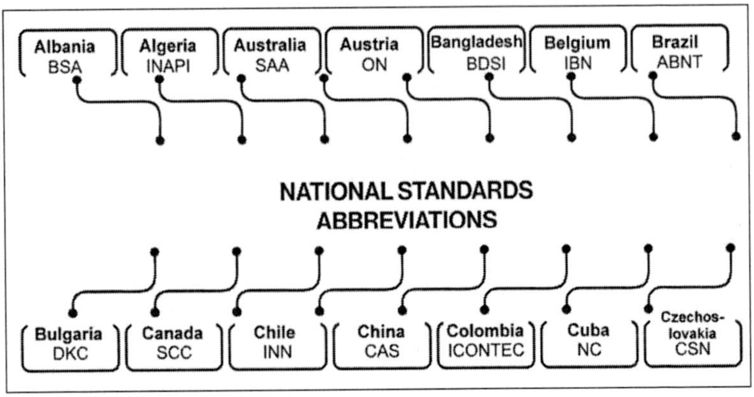
Albania BSA
Algeria INAPI
Australia SAA
Austria ON
Bangladesh BDSI
Belgium IBN
Brazil ABNT
NATIONAL STANDARDS ABBREVIATIONS
Bulgaria DKC
Canada SCC
Chile INN
China CAS
Colombia ICONTEC
Cuba NC
Czechos-lovakia CSN

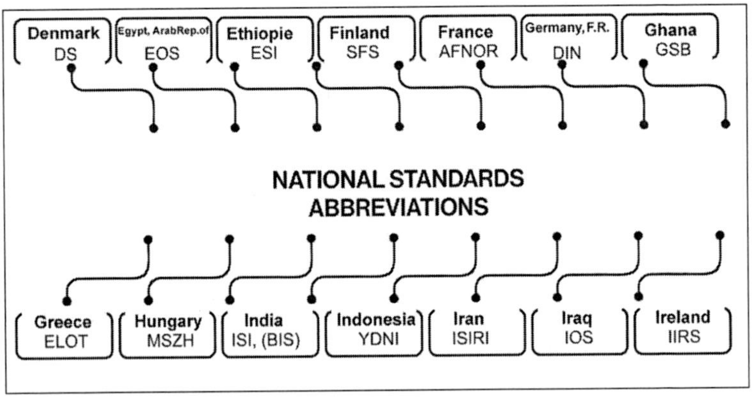
Denmark DS
Egypt, ArabRep.of EOS
Ethiopie ESI
Finland SFS
France AFNOR
Germany, F.R. DIN
Ghana GSB
NATIONAL STANDARDS ABBREVIATIONS
Greece ELOT
Hungary MSZH
India ISI, (BIS)
Indonesia YDNI
Iran ISIRI
Iraq IOS
Ireland IIRS

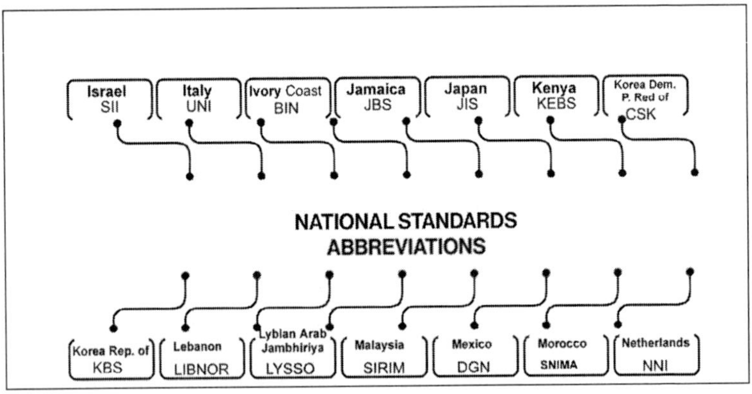
Israel SII
Italy UNI
Ivory Coast BIN
Jamaica JBS
Japan JIS
Kenya KEBS
Korea Dem. P. Red of CSK
NATIONAL STANDARDS ABBREVIATIONS
Korea Rep. of KBS
Lebanon LIBNOR
Lyblan Arab Jambhiriya LYSSO
Malaysia SIRIM
Mexico DGN
Morocco SNIMA
Netherlands NNI

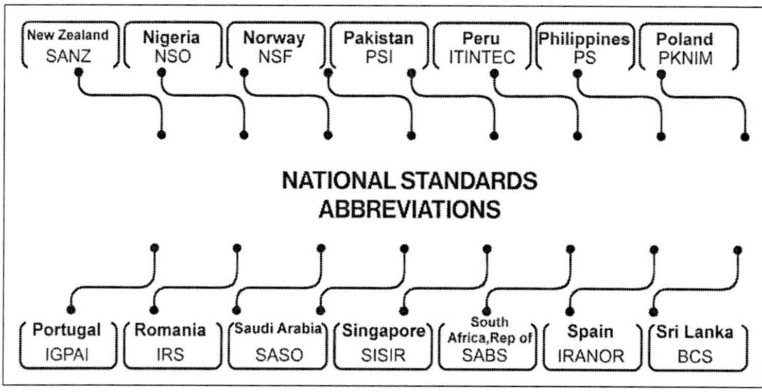

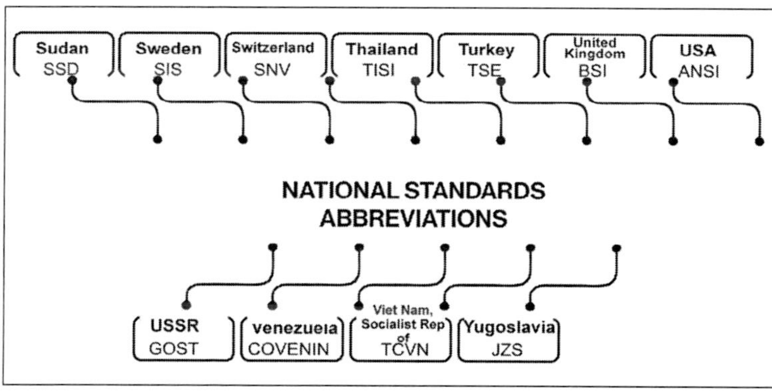

These standards ensure compatibility and reliability of fasteners across different sectors and regions. By adhering to them, manufacturers and users can maintain quality assurance, reduce risks of failure, and meet regulatory compliance requirements.

Chapter 6

Common Misconceptions About Fasteners and Their Impact

Despite being the unsung heroes behind every machine, structure, and appliance, fasteners remain one of the most misunderstood components in manufacturing.

Myths and misconceptions, ranging from the simplicity of their production to the idea that "all fasteners are the same," have long obstructed the Indian fastener industry's path to global excellence.

These outdated beliefs not only diminish the perceived value of quality fasteners but also lead to poor procurement decisions, costly failures, and missed opportunities for innovation.

Busting these myths is not just about setting the record straight—

It's about unlocking new levels of efficiency, consistency, performance, and profitability.

By understanding the science, precision, and innovation that go into making world-class fasteners, let us together pave the way for an industry that is not only competitive globally but is also a cornerstone of India's manufacturing strength.

Let's begin to bust one myth at a time –

1. "Fasteners Can Be Made Easily"

The Lie: Fasteners are perceived as simple components that require minimal expertise or equipment.

The Truth: Fasteners are precision-engineered components that demand advanced manufacturing knowledge and stringent quality controls. A leading white goods manufacturer faced frequent assembly failures due to low-quality imported fasteners with improper threading and inconsistent hardness. We redesigned their fasteners using precise thread rolling and heat treatment, leading to seamless assembly and zero delays.

2. "It Does Not Take Time to Manufacture Fasteners"

The Lie: Many believe fasteners can be produced quickly, ignoring the complex processes involved.

The Truth: Manufacturing fasteners involves at least 10 critical stages, each contributing to the final product's performance and reliability. Processes include wire drawing for seamless wire, cold forging for structural integrity, thread rolling for precise dimensional standards, heat treatment for controlled hardness and tensile strength, and surface coating for enhanced durability and corrosion resistance. Every step demands careful calibration, specialized tooling, and rigorous quality checks to comply with global standards like BIS, ISO, DIN, JIS, etc. Rushing through these phases can lead to flaws such as brittle threads, uneven coatings, or inconsistent hardness.

For example, a customer once shared that due to an incomplete coating process at their vendor's end, they had to recall 5,000 machines from the market.

The skipped process resulted in corrosion, leading to penalties, rework at their warehouse, and field repairs at customer sites.

The vendor was also blacklisted, tarnishing their reputation.

Market recalls are a significant risk, underscoring why fastener production demands time and precision.

3. "Indian Manufacturers Cut Corners to Save Costs"

The Lie: It is often assumed that Indian manufacturers compromise quality to remain cost-effective.

The Truth: Cost efficiency does not equate to cutting corners. Reputable Indian manufacturers adhere to stringent global standards such as BIS, ISO, and IATF to ensure unmatched quality. This commitment includes investing in high-grade raw materials, state-of-the-art machinery, and comprehensive quality control systems.

Fasteners undergo hardness and tensile testing, corrosion resistance analysis, and dimensional checks at various stages of production.

Unlike many imported manufacturers, we have invested heavily in backward integration, performing all processes under one roof, from wire drawing to plating. This ensures consistency and quality, positioning us at par with global players in the industry.

4. "Indian Manufacturers Do Not Have the Capacity"

The Lie: Some believe Indian manufacturers cannot meet the high-volume demands of industries like automotive and construction.

The Truth with an Example: An automotive OEM required a large order of screws and doubted the Indian manufacturers' ability to handle the volume while maintaining quality.

Leveraging our daily production capacity of 20 million screws, we fulfilled their order within the stipulated time, adhering to strict IATF standards.

Streamlined operations and a robust supply chain proved that Indian manufacturers can meet even the most demanding orders efficiently.

5. "Indian Manufacturers Do Not Have the Technology to Compete with Imported Fasteners"

The Lie: Imported fasteners are often seen as more advanced due to perceived technological superiority.

The Truth: Indian manufacturers utilize cutting-edge technology, including CNC machinery, automated production lines, and precision inspection systems, to produce fasteners that rival global competitors. Our in-house testing facilities include advanced equipment for tensile testing, fatigue analysis, and salt spray testing, ensuring every product meets or exceeds international benchmarks.

Our fully integrated facility, starting from raw material processing to coating and complemented by advanced testing, provides us with the perfect edge to compete globally.

6. "All Fasteners Are the Same"

The Lie: Fasteners are often perceived as interchangeable, with no significant difference between products from various manufacturers.

The Truth: Fasteners differ widely in material composition, tensile strength, surface coatings, and thread geometry. For example, an automotive fastener designed to withstand high vibration and temperature differs significantly from a modular furniture fastener optimized for aesthetic finishes and light load applications.

Using a generic fastener risks assembly failures, reduced product lifespan, and compromised safety.

For instance, we developed a fastener for a customer that reduced the manpower required for assembly from two operators to one by optimizing the thread profile.

The result? Reduced labor costs and improved productivity.

7. "Fasteners Are Cheap and Should Be Priced That Way"

The Lie: Many customers perceive fasteners as low-cost commodities that don't justify significant investment.

The Truth: The cost of fasteners reflects the quality of materials, precision in manufacturing, and adherence to stringent testing standards. Opting for low-cost fasteners may save a few pennies upfront, but can result in costly repercussions, such as assembly line downtime, product recalls, or severe damage to brand reputation.

Fasteners typically account for less than 1% of total assembly costs, yet they can contribute to 100% of product failures.

A stark example of this is the Shivaji statue in Maharashtra, which collapsed just eight months after its installation. Investigations revealed that ordinary iron bolts, prone to rust, were used instead of rust-resistant materials. This catastrophic failure occurred despite the statue's construction costing ₹2.44 crores*, underscoring the dangers of compromising on fastener quality.

* *Source: https://www.newslaundry.com/2024/08/27/shivaji-statue-collapse-rushed-project-rusted-bolts-and-unpaid-bills*

8. "Fasteners Don't Contribute to Innovation"

The Lie: Fasteners are often seen as static, unchanging components with no scope for innovation.

The Truth: The fastener industry is a hub of innovation, with advancements in materials, coatings, and designs tailored to modern demands. For instance, self-drilling screws save installation time in construction by eliminating pre-drilling, while anti-vibration fasteners are essential in automotive and aerospace applications to ensure safety and performance.

Partnering with an innovative manufacturer can lead to customized solutions that enhance efficiency and reliability in specific applications.

9. "Lead Times Are the Same Across Manufacturers"

The Lie: Customers often assume that all fastener suppliers deliver within similar time frames.

The Truth: Lead times vary significantly depending on a manufacturer's production capacity, in-house capabilities, and supply chain efficiency. Manufacturers with integrated operations, such as ours, can produce and deliver fasteners faster, thanks to streamlined processes like in-house testing, automated threading, and efficient logistics.

For example, while standard manufacturers might take weeks, we have fulfilled urgent OEM orders within two days without compromising quality.

On-time delivery is critical to preventing line stoppages and supply chain disruptions.

10. "Fastener Suppliers Don't Offer Customization"

The Lie: It's a common misconception that fastener suppliers only provide off-the-shelf products.

The Truth: Reputable manufacturers offer tailored solutions to meet specific application needs, from customized dimensions and thread pitches to special coatings and materials.

For example, an AC manufacturer required screws with a specific coating to match their product aesthetics. By providing a tailored solution, we enhanced their product's appearance.

Customization ensures compatibility, reliability, and optimal performance, especially for critical applications.

All these myths that I have busted here are not just tall claims, but on-ground feedback and testimonies from clients that testify to these truths.

Trust & Reliability Without a Doubt

When it comes to fasteners, Raj Industries **stands out for its consistency and reliability**. Their **in-house capabilities and rigorous quality control processes** made them our go-to partner for years. The team **always delivers on time**, no matter how challenging the requirements are. It's rare to find a company that **truly understands the critical role of fasteners and consistently delivers solutions you can trust**.

Not just Manufacturing Fasteners but Providing Solutions that Impact!

Having worked with Dhruv Khandelwal & Raj Industries for several years, **I can confidently say he is one of the most knowledgeable and reliable individuals I've met in the fasteners industry**.

His ability to solve complex challenges, coupled with his deep understanding of manufacturing processes, made him an invaluable partner.

What sets him apart is **his integrity and dedication**—he genuinely cares about delivering the best for his clients.

He doesn't just sell fasteners; he provides solutions that make a difference.

Chapter 7

C Fasteners = Efficiency, Not Just Fixing

In the world of Original Equipment Manufacturing (OEM), the fastener may be the smallest component, but it has the power to make or break the entire product.

Often overlooked in the design phase, the right fastener, and more importantly, the right fastener partner, can be the catalyst for extraordinary transformation in efficiency, performance, and profitability.

From reducing assembly time and maintenance costs to improving aesthetics and enabling innovation, precision-engineered fasteners play a critical role at every stage of an OEM's journey.

Collaborating with a proactive and technically adept fastener manufacturer can turn everyday production challenges into competitive advantages, helping OEMs stay ahead in an increasingly demanding and quality-conscious market. Here's how you, as an OEM, can not only optimize but also maximize your success.

1. Custom Engineering is the Key to Enhanced Performance

The Problem: Many OEMs assume that standard fasteners will work across all applications. However, different industries require unique fastener designs to optimize performance, durability, and ease of assembly. Using generic fasteners can lead to frequent replacements, misalignment, or assembly inefficiencies.

The Solution: Custom-engineered fasteners address these challenges by tailoring head types, thread profiles, and coatings to the specific requirements of the application.

- **Example:** We worked with a white goods OEM struggling with loose screws in high-vibration environments. By designing a self-locking thread, we eliminated the need for additional adhesives, reducing assembly time and improving reliability.
- **Outcome:** Improved performance, cost savings on adhesives, and increased product durability.

2. Fastener Quality Directly Impacts Assembly Line Efficiency

The Problem: Inadequate fasteners cause delays in assembly lines due to thread misalignment, tool jamming, or inconsistent dimensions. This results in increased downtime, additional labor costs, and rejected components.

The Solution: High-precision manufacturing and a suitable fastener for the application

- **Example:** An assembly line worker told us, 'Every time I had to oil these screws, it felt like a waste of time.' By redesigning the thread, we removed that step entirely, saving thousands of hours annually for the company.
- **Outcome: Faster assembly, reduced manual labor, improved efficiency, and lower operational costs.**

3. Advanced Coatings Reduce Long-Term Maintenance Costs

The Problem: Standard fasteners often corrode or wear out prematurely, leading to frequent maintenance and warranty claims. Many OEMs underestimate how coatings impact longevity.

The Solution: Specialized coatings, such as zinc-nickel, zinc-aluminium flake, enhance corrosion resistance, reduce friction, and extend product life.

- **Example:** A white goods manufacturer had screws rusting inside washing machines. We provided **zinc nickel-coated fasteners**, which extended the corrosion resistance from 200 **hours to 500+ hours in salt spray tests**.
- **Outcome: Increased product lifespan and improved brand reputation.**

4. In-House Testing Eliminates Hidden Defects

The Problem: Some fastener defects—like micro-cracks or improper heat treatment—are invisible during visual inspections. These defects can lead to failures in critical applications.

The Solution: In-house testing facilities ensure 100% defect-free products before dispatch.

- **Example:** A construction OEM faced repeated complaints of screw heads snapping under load. Our in-house microstructure and hardness testing identified an inconsistency in material processing, which we corrected by refining the heat treatment process.

- **Outcome:** Zero **failures post-implementation, reducing field service costs.**

5. Smaller Design Adjustments Can Lead to Big Cost Savings

The Problem: Fastener design is often overlooked as a cost-saving opportunity. Minor inefficiencies in fastener selection can lead to material waste, unnecessary labor, and excess tooling costs.

The Solution: Optimizing fastener design can reduce material usage and simplify assembly.

- **Example:** An OEM reduced assembly time by switching from Phillips-head to another drive, improving grip and reducing slippage.
- **Outcome: Assembly efficiency increased by 20%, and tool wear decreased by 15%.**

6. Corrosion Starts from the Inside Out

The Problem: Many OEMs focus on external coatings for corrosion protection but neglect how rust can begin inside fastener threads, under coatings, or within assembly interfaces. Additionally, when the coating of the mating part and the fastener differ, electrochemical reactions can accelerate corrosion, leading to premature wear and potential damage to the mating component.

The Solution: Proper corrosion prevention starts with material selection, internal thread coatings, and ensuring that the coatings of mating parts and fasteners are compatible to prevent galvanic corrosion.

- **Example:** A manufacturer using zinc-coated screws in an powder coated aluminum assembly observed accelerated corrosion where the two materials met. We introduced zinc-aluminum coated fasteners, preventing electrochemical reactions and protecting both the fastener and the mating part.
- **Outcome: Product lifespan extended by 55%, reducing maintenance costs and preventing damage to mating components.**

7. Supplier Collaboration Can Drive Product Innovation

The Problem: OEMs often treat fastener suppliers as mere vendors rather than innovation partners.

The Solution: Early supplier collaboration enables unique design solutions that enhance product performance.

- **Example:** We integrated two parts into a single fastener for a manufacturer, increasing their production efficiency by 35% and eliminating one component from their system.
- **Outcome: Faster assembly time and increased production**

8. Fasteners Influence Aesthetics and End-User Experience

The Problem: OEMs often overlook the visual and functional impact of fasteners on the final product.

The Solution: Selecting the right fastener finish and design enhances aesthetics and user satisfaction.

- **Example:** A premium appliance brand used stainless steel fasteners with polished heads, enhancing product appearance.
- **Outcome: Improved consumer perception and brand value.**

9. Preventative Maintenance Starts with the Right Fastener

The Problem: Hard-to-remove fasteners increase maintenance costs, downtime, and the likelihood of damaging surrounding components. When fasteners wear out too quickly, frequent replacements add to overall servicing expenses.

The Solution: Fasteners designed for easy removal and reusability improve serviceability, reducing both maintenance effort and cost. Using dual-drive fasteners (e.g., hex flange head screws with a Philips drive) allows for better torque control and extended usability.

- **Example:** An OEM switched from standard screws to hex head screws, enabling the after-service executive to reuse the fastener 10 times instead of just 3 times without compromising integrity.
- **Outcome: Reduced fastener waste, lower maintenance costs, and faster service times improve overall product lifecycle efficiency.**

10. Packaging Affects Efficiency and Corrosion Protection

The Problem: Poor packaging can lead to rusting, misplacement, or damaged fasteners, affecting assembly efficiency and increasing rejection rates. Exposure to moisture, improper stacking, and weak packaging materials can compromise fastener integrity before they even reach the production line.

The Solution: Effective packaging ensures that fasteners arrive in perfect condition, free from corrosion or physical damage.

- **Moisture Control:** Desiccant packets absorb excess moisture, keeping the internal environment dry.
- **Airtight Sealing:** Packaging that prevents exposure to oxygen and moisture eliminates the primary causes of rust.
- **Moisture-Resistant Materials:** Using polyethylene bags of 60+ microns thickness protects against humidity and condensation.
- **Impact Protection:** Durable, organized packaging prevents thread damage and facilitates easy identification.
- **Stackable & Labeled Packaging:** Optimized packaging design reduces assembly line delays by enabling quick access and preventing fastener misplacement.
- **Example:** A client faced rust-related rejects due to inadequate packaging. We introduced desiccant packets in each polybag and laminated the packaging for enhanced moisture protection. In another case, changing the packaging shape eliminated thread damage during transportation and storage.
- **Outcome: Zero rust-related issues, reduced handling time, and smoother production flow.**

Chapter 8

Stay Connected

Congratulations on completing this book!

This book was written to **shift your perspective**—fasteners are not just small components, but essential drivers of manufacturing success. A single screw can make or break an assembly line, influence product performance, and impact an entire supply chain.

Have you ensured your fastener choices align with your production goals? If not, now is the time to rethink your approach.

The right fastener choice today prevents costly failures tomorrow.

If you have any questions, feedback, or simply want to discuss fasteners in more detail, I'd love to hear from you. You can write to me at **dkhandelwal@rajindscrews.com.**

I'd be delighted to walk the path of OEM success as your growth partner.

Stay connected at

LinkedIn: www.linkedin.com/in/dhruvkhandelwal27

LinkedIn: https://linkedin.com/company/raj-industries-malakpur/

Instagram: raj_industries_malakpur

Website: www.rajindustriesfasteners.com